1

The withering endless roaming terraces
Of doom and gloom goes as far and
wide as the Contempt shown
by our rulers,
A fog that will never die
A sun that will never lye
This is the jailhouse and you are my
Keeper , desperate towns of Britain
Decay into annihilation , the Christmases
Are dank and the summers are dark ,
the youth only find faith in a rope,
While they sedate and tranquilize the masses
to have there way, victims create victims
In a brutal endless cycle that shall
Never have no end
The faces are sad all the good times been had
Now there is no way,
For now there is no way

Its not raining but it may as well be the English weather

Somehow reflects the peoples moods at moments. I a

Mere peasant and millions more in this "Austerity"

climate am reminded our role and sole purpose is to work

The most unrewarding medial jobs, gain debt get sold on

The ideology of family and be imprisoned in an inesca-

Ble hell where your only option is waiting to be of Part of

The daily deceased . The conventional family has just

Been all but decimated disaffected by material marketing

To All there surroundings while The ghettos of non-
opportunity Spring up everywhere . Children running -

around naked In the street while the mother is haggard ask-
ing The doctor For more sedation while selling amphetamines

To Random risky clients knocking at her unfortunate door.

The male customers are similar to that of cavemen—the

Average person would be eaten alive by these people. That's

What they do: They prey on vulnerability and they don't
even realise it to themselves because this northern town has a

A notorious abuse level, sub education level, and a lack of

of compassion has resulted in a heartless population who

are trained and are now immune to the rest of the world

Like it just doesn't exist . They speak in a dialect

That makes broken English look like the queens English.

Cruelty is the order of the day it's the only sense of power

They have left . We are always in a permanent midst of

An epidemic of large numbers of our youth hanging them

selves because they don't see a way out of this depraved

Cess-pit town . And they are forgotten about as quick as

The horrendous act its self, told with the same voice as they

Present the weather report in. Just another broken heart with no place to go. You can hardly blame anyone for taking the nearest intoxicant to escape this impossible economical cage. Everything costs MONEY (correction everything costs a hell of a lot of money). The majority of the population haven't gone beyond the end of there town, in some cases streets. The youth look aggressive yet dragged they know what is in store for them. Thank god there is no easy access to guns because everyday we'd all be dead. Middle aged men prey on children and young girls , if you ask a girl her first sexual experience it usually was some kind of trap or involve some element of humiliation with a man 20 plus years her senior . After a lot of damage sets in its hard to see the light in people's eyes, there is always a lingering sense of total forthcoming dread. School breaks the child's spirit , its just a place where legally the children here have to go. Every teacher in my time was bitter and

Took pleasure in breaking certain individuals. The lack of any
Kind of compassion has been drilled out of society as I

Currently write there is a man down slumtown who is obviously at his lowest ebb. He's scaled a high building getting ready for the his final Painful moment on earth and there is a crowd of 7 people somehow rising of alleged human beings shouting shrieking at him that he's a "coward" and " needs to jump so I can capture It" on their soulless phones. Sometimes I think mobile phones Should only be useable only in emergency circumstances. I don't think human beings were genetically engineered to be inconstant communication. What kind of wiring would provoke a reaction like that we shall establish. Lets unveil the tragedies Westminster has caused that haven't been news worthy or just criminally covered up. The television portrays that every paedophile is working class or an over the hill working class celeb an now portraying young Muslim males as predators. Even a top Police detective was recorded saying "We can't go gallivanting round Westminster and arrest serving politicians". Which is obvious blatant corruption and spits in the face of any form of democracy. The ITV news starts with one of its most crooked creatures stating an outright denial of underage sex allegations with Royalty & Geoffrey Epstein, where else would you witness something like this than an out & out dictatorship. But your average person is just struggling to get by let alone try an implement any kind of change. These rings are so embedded and self

Self protecting that penetrating them is impossible with out any kind of amnesty for people to come forward who cant live with themselves. Its a playground for abuse here kids roam the streets past midnight , there is no concept of love and the internet specifically Facebook is a paedophiles dream. We've all seen the stings but they are the needles in haystacks the real 13 year old doesn't stand a chance. Its not the "working class" paedophile who is creating this demand its people like the prime minister's top advisor, the high court judge , the lawmakers who will imprison an almost joke post office robber out of desperation of debt for 10 years and then give a child rapist 7 years…

Its shows where there true priories' lay. We also have the strictest libel laws in the world to stop any naming and shaming which has to be amended. The kids aspire to violence here, not for any kind of sport or past time , Curb Stomping some poor soul. It's hate crime central where you find a lack of education and culture cultivates ignorance manifesting in irrational hatred

- How dare you become a woman ? Being one of many many bigoted ideologies and lifestyles that result in heart-breaking tragedy .Well some "Real" men stomped him to death down

- A dark ignorant road I went down every day growing up. "Good on yer" is the reason why, I feel so alone in this world some times. Girls killing themselves because they don't meet a mans predetermined image of what a woman

Should be. The church I was indoctrinated into and actually believed was good until it turned out to be an "abuse mafia". I hated going to church as a child, the pomp and ceremony never made sense to me. One Sunday at the age of 6 I screamed at my mother in our small bungalow "I'm not going to church! GOD ISNT REAL". My mother scolded me and said now I was definantly going to hell. So I grabbed the nearest crayon being purple an wrote on my wallpaper " god is not real" . I was locked in my room whilst the rest of my family went to the ritual. I guess I was hell bound now. My school was a mixture of sadism and humiliation with me being interviewed about whether a child in my small class had been head-butted or whether the teacher was trying to get in his face and make him flinch. . It was a repetitive diatribe this particular teacher would start his lessons by informing us because of our backgrounds and education we would be working in a fecal factory and not to expect much fro life. Music was my saviour but even now psychedelic/postpunk/electro/blues has all been relegated to the status and importance as model railway collections, thanks to the culture secretary and the drones who should be managing tesco running the music labels. If you have anything to say , forget it. Now people have been pre-conditioned to like synthetic empty shallow beats with crass lyrics which tend to fuel fire on ignorance/bigotry or simply stupidity. People will just go with any flock regardless , Similar to vilifying a total faith they buy the entire

Non-Muslim threat in all our western communities. There the "New" communists . TV ,Radio which is obviously so staged managed its embarrassing, just so we can keep the illegal occupation of the east going. We've lost our culture quite frankly we have lost our way. The crimes are becoming more an more depraved. My family is beyond broken I haven't spent a Christmas with my family in almost 15 years and I'm 30. Everything has been dumbed down to make us all sub –servient and unable to think for ourselves anymore. Nobody wants to look foolish so striking up a conversation with a stranger is like a "paranoia exchange" . Everyone is a perceived threat. There is only one thriving economy and that is hard drugs, it stimulates the economy, it creates jobs and there is a dope dealer on almost every street. The youth have the options of –Sell Drugs, Work a job where you can barely get by, Or have kids to claim benefits that are now becoming history. Sell dope go to jail or suicide out of desperation. There is no hope here, brothels exist on many run down streets. Many girls just striving to keep themselves alive with drugs. The houses always take the cut because all the money is usually spent on drugs. These exist on all manor of streets some rougher and grimier than others I'm not referring to escorts or the horrendous sex trafficking that goes on but if you sleep with either you have just paid for rape. The average copper on the street treat them as vermin even though they probably wouldn't have a job without them. These officers are so ignorant and thick they can't even realise this cycle even when a girl is

Annually murdered yearly. This town shall always be a dope town and now we're paying the price of that with an underclass that can't even articulate how they feel or how to even speak to people in mainstream society. Stories of someone I know taking in a street girl and he kept all the money in his house for rent & such under his pillow as she slept in his spare room. When he awoke the money was of course long gone so he confronted her : she immediately attacked him head butted him and broke his spectacles. He was being a nice guy he wasn't looking for sex but its sometimes hard to remember that this girl Is a victim herself . It's a sad cycle but in this town thou shall become a victim. Victims create victims because there is no way these people can even comprehend the guilt that they should feel, but sadly they never will. Ed Milliband is our local MP believe it or not and his "constituency office" if you could call it that is just a billboard with no visible entry with dusty cob-webbed dusty rusty steel cages apparently for windows. Iv never even seen him here not once just a sign saying that he is our elected member of parliament. As I've stated hate crimes are rife to the point that as I suspect with a lot of people : they lead a double life, Sometimes to that individual shameful. "Bob" was as straight as they come with tattoos, racist comments and usual bigotry baggage. Until he was found in front of a video camera dead from hanging dressed head to toe completely in drag and make up. Obviously after receiving his last orgasm he slipped on that fine -line. It was a blow and shock for the hard men in the pub and his funeral was a very toned down affair. With non of his so called good friends attending .

Its still respectable to be racist here and some people to be rascist here and some people are offended if you aren't , I was almost ousted from a cab just because I wouldn't say "yes your right" . You have to be defiant to survive here one sign of weakness and you're a goner. People get stabbed over the most absurd reasons and circumstances. The local authoritys and mayors office are no better people behaving like gangsters as they stole thousands and thousands from the towns redevelopment budget money. They literarily took it and ran! Abroad and in a swiss bank account 'oh doncatraz how your venom drips into every facet'. The worst establishment criminals it seems get waiting list as time goes by the government are going to just wait for the most wicked despicable deviants to die without facing any kind of real trial and justice. As well as iv already stated an officer from operation yewtree has been quoted as saying "oh we're not going to go gallivanting round Westminster." Which absolutely says it all. Just non connected yesteryear celebrities abusers meet the wrath, fed to the lions to bate the baying mob. " Historical abuse" - which minimises these horrific atrocities, Kind of shows you whose side there on.

This is like any other day we all want change but under no circumstances will people come together. One man's liberty is another man's police state but when it comes to children we should all be united on children otherwise we really are inhuman now.

I am asked for change from EVERYBODY 99% of the time- not even homeless this is the culture of the town and am sure its spreading far and wide. There is zero shame in their mind its shame on you for caring in their eyes. As a child this was relent- less getting to school was a constant struggle with every fiend imaginable preying on all the children it was treacherous. One of the worst offenders there in his mind spaced and gone at 8..am predatorily preying on school girls would always be ready to pounce in this grimy shelter called a "bus station". Once after school I met my mum and this Jamaican crack fiend was sexual- ly assaulting the young teens the degenerate was dressed in the most bizarre bandana that I doubt shall ever be repeated. It was a yellow and black 90's Netto carrier bag wrapped covering the top of his intoxicated skull. He was leaning heavily on a clearly intimidated girl. When my mother stepped in and told him to leave her alone "Suck My Cock Bitch!!!" was his only reply de- mented eyes. I have always found it quite staggering that crystal meth has never really taken off in the uk unlike the epidemic propositions we saw with crack cocaine and heroin inevitably did in the 80s 90s. The cost of that kind of enormous magnitude in just all the public services alone yet again the raw street level rabid criminality just on society in general has always seemed to me a slight 'fishy'. As those 2 devastating drugs hit the western world extremely altering the class system in the UK and US , England was enthralled in a bitter war of the dismantling in the mining industry. The minor's families starved and their sons had

Zero hope and then straight out the midst comes this almost class cleansing drug . But its quite questionable even today the constant regular over availability of obtaining heroin & crack but never really meth-amphetamine. To me it kind of shows me who really calls the shots. Black untraceable funds are very use-full to any faction criminal or state and there's no business like dope business , rain or shine. Currently I'm just waiting for the next , there's not many of us left 4 boys left in my class of boys at school and I've not even touched 30! Drunken hangings completely voiceless and hopeless . I think a LOT of us have felt this way where it seems all life does is make us suffer and there is no shining way out. The notion today saying a "cowards way out" seems such an ignorant statement for someone to say , they have no concept of life other than there ignorant own. Its beyond all our recognitions to literally take our lives in our hands and feel the feeling as death sets in . In a lot of cases people may take overdoses but they do it as a statement or a point in life they cannot get beyond. Once your foot leaves that stool and that rope zips under your jaw line its just too late you can't call for help. You can't cry out for help as you dangle with a rope separating your spine with your own weight , it's a totally un-addressed epidemic especially in young people why? It would seem our political masters obviously don't care and even In some kind of miracle they can't change the ghetto benefit life-style that's been economically implemented . If the average person knew what went on in esteemed authorities institutions

They'd be outraged. An underclass is being exploited and all kinds of unprecedented atrocities that are swept under the filthy rug. Because its bad for business and the mentality just like a business is protect the institution not the victims. It can drive you crazy if you let it . They have successfully dismantled working class culture , its done there is no community now. They have to have you in a constant state of anxiety and fear to pull half the scams on you. Everyone has hit hard times and you can see the desperation in every awful act you see and hear. Stealing is just the main profession and trade in this town. Taking advantage is another . If you show any kind of kindness you shall be spat out flying round the world. You can see it as out of towners depart from trains and are immediately pounced on with a dire patter as they are hounded into submission and then try for the double as they either grab the wallet or even the luggage. Everyones health is in a constant state of near fatal decay for many reasons . Growing up as a child in the 90's pub boom I remember a bouncer was prosecuted for sleeping with unknowing females as he was in stages of full blown aids . It always turned my stomach he was a bouncer at the towns biggest clubs and spread it around out of ignorance or an irrational anger at the world. Makes me sad and angry the daily incidents/ atrocities. I've heard the horrendous primal howl when someone is informed of the worst news you could ever hear vibrating through your body and out into your soul for eternity. A five year old girl lays dying as a young man in a citron flees the

Scene . The driver left as if the girl caused the horrendous accident without a care in the world. This is sadly not the first and unfortunately not the last. One of the more despicable professions in this town is "clairvoyants" there not even good scam artists here they just prey on the bereaved and lonely in a painfully obvious manner. Widows already hooked on substances designed to change your brain chemisty and for years as we all know can in some cases make enough changes to cause suicide, live in deep depression that is exasperated by doctors who believe its easier to dope somebody up to the eyeballs on Amatrptaline than to actually care for them and do the long haul of therapy of talking and going through it with the victim. One woman I knew was left alone with 5 kids and was clearly being completely played and defrauded showing me pictures of her deceased husbands ghost as I just see a picture just of standard light reflection off of lenses. But its been "verified" by these corpse thieves in the night. She is being preyed upon like many in this country mixed with psych-drugs they are psychologically extorted both combined are a recipe for opportunist disaster. These merchants of lies are literal low lives. As she says her dead husband has even more messages for her but hey always leave them with a 'cliffhanger' but at a break neck price for the true content of course. Widowed I hear her life has descended into chaos selling speed to all comers to make the payments and mounting debt. Even the state are taking advantage loan sharking to the most vulnerable minimum paid workers who really

Like some special demographic of scum with nuclear interest. She walks around in a daze kids raising themselves barely clothed with every terrible local character walking through her open door policy . Anything could happen & everything did happen. The children become desensitised and a numbness sets in where communication is distorted to almost a primal converse. The children in the town take the worst toll becoming sociopathic as that's all they see. Two young children commit the worst attempted murder since the appalling case of James Bulger case. It was the only reason this politically neglected wasteland received national news. The two brothers were like so many typical of the town. They would spend days sat watching hardcore pornography with their father smoking cannabis resin most days. In between them watching there parents having sex right in front of them on the living room floor on a Saturday night. How those brave boys who were beaten, burned, and sexually assaulted survived I shall never know. The head officer on the case said he stopped the assault on the half dead child simply out of being tired. It's a cancer that shall always possess this town until kingdom government done. I think everyone as a child assumes things shall be better when they grow up, but if you haven't escaped your class then you are stranded by design. Everyone fantasises about some kind of escapism when they know the demon shall always be waiting for them. The local authorities , government even ed millibands rinky-dink almost criminal front office wont do anything about it. They obviously

Don't care that middle aged woman in storming debt are throwing themselves from tower blocks. It doesn't fit into their stage managed politics. Kids vanish into the care system , where do they go? Where are the stats and numbers? Everyone's too distracted by the latest flashy BS or simply trying to survive. A withering woman is getting by spending what little money she has on bupane gas of all things. I have felt the effects of many substances but this is not one of them . Cans and cans would litter her house onto poverty stricken oblivion . She eventually grabbed a cigarette and inevitably set herself into a human torch. The whole bottom floor went up. This economical cleansing that has spawned this hell does have hell to pay. The only representation is on morning freak shows under a false pretence of "we're saving families" . Even though the shows entire premise is to tear families apart through lie detectors , these bent tyrants need to learn these people are victims of terrible economical governing and attacking them for things that happen every day is a despicable act . They look like patients wheeled out in the bedlam for the entertainment purposes it genuinely leaves you feeling dirty. The whole system is set up against them even articulation they simply don't stand a chance. How bad is it going to get? With an entire town no being able to articulate English? But just grunt like animals. Young people killed in droves , old people treated like useless draing cattle and its going to get worse . Many have sank into a deep depression leading to the great regression like we all know all the good times have been

Anti-deppresents mess with and distort your brain chemistry to vegetise you into hollow highs and dangerous lows no matter what the new wonder drug is. Because after all its easier to dope them to the gills than care for them. Its always baffled me that someone who is suicidal would be given a substance that could make them commit suicide. Life has been made frustrating held hostage to non-consensual future where people are becoming more cold and non violent sociopaths are living in a desperate climate. You can't even talk to anyone in your life because they simply just don't have the tolerance . The head lose chicken till you drain of life and drop is a trap we all live by . We've all lost our community spirit which banded us all together as one greater family. Drugs has mainly destroyed that and as we've spoken it creates jobs it stimulates economy and contributes to supposed government policing budgets. The loss of that community spirit and compassion which brings hope where there otherwise isn't. Propaganda litters the television, i.e. you should hate, gypsys/travellers anyone on state benefits, the Romanian beggers, and now disgustingly the homeless. Where the conservative party want to make it illegall to be homeless in London. How ridiculous and out of touch do they sound. As these self righteous pathetic little men who don't have to wipe there own backside due to their ENDLESS expenses, this is not a joke its not anything its criminal. If you or I used defrauded the tax office and bought a second home or "hardcore literature" or any other of their deviancy we'd be fired and arrested.

People have had enough of being completely economically-socially abused and left with the imprint that you don't matter they are totally devalued. Sections within the police sadly are becoming the new criminal gang behaving like the LAPD than your good old bobby on the beat. I grew up like many that the police were always the good guys no matter the circumstances, coming to my school to take all our DNA as iv figured out growing up. That's the hope we show in our youth.

I see the police picking on the defenceless all the time they really are mercenaries , there either like gangsters themselves or like old SS guards saying "im only doing my job" . The vetting is a joke recollections of a behind closed doors nazi who had made officer. The recruitment should be far more psychological and stringent. Psychological evacuations need to be made because there is nothing worse than a bully in a uniform . But it usually is the local bully in uniform who takes the most liberty's

With you. The first time I ever had any interactions with the police I was damn borderline molested, I just despise in anyone who relishes in anyone feel small. Middle Englands got to wake up to all these things and stop being so apathetic to this cancer spreading through every facet of our society. Otherwise we'.re not gonna have one anymore which im sure is the design: dismantle working class culture. Dumb the masses down through all forms of media till they accept absolutely anything you spoon feed them.

We need real hardship centres not horrible shelters with no beds . Hardship centres where there is professionals and rehabilitation not just from drugs, rehab for lifestyles as that's what's the root of this problem-changing negative destructive behavioural patterns. But there's more money to be made by criminalising these victims then actually showing them a better way. But the greed of the conservative government or 99.9% of all governments knows no bounds. Social workers who can't tell the difference between "becoming emotionally invested" and simply not giving a hoot or the new bread of police officer who is blinded by power and doesn't understand how people become in their minds "vermin" . They believe there beating up the "bad guys" (oh if life was just as simple as that) when there the worst guys of the bunch. I admire the genius of methodical investigator going after online predators and paedophile rings. But the guys on the beat just try an make everyone who isn't business class feel small. Not remembering drugs and alcohol are always waiting for you. Its only now being recognised as a mental disease . When I was growing up it was looked upon as they were the lowest of the low. They would be out casted from their families like that would improve matters they were outcasted from mainstream society. Being disowned by all their families would only lead them to one place : The Street. Where no one cared a jot they were abused in the streets beaten by almost all sections of society. There health was completely disregarded, they would literally lose everything.

There was nothing more heartbreaking for me than watching a young 20 year old being wheeled down the street by her junkie co-dependent "lover" in a wheelchair after obviously after having her leg amputated from a bad missed shot to her leg. Its very risky business if a shot is missed in the femerarol artery and if a shot is missed can lead to a deadly blood cot or total amputation of the leg. I saw the dead look in this poor girls eyes there was no light no more all her dreams seemingly now snuffed out by a demon that only takes residence in our deprived wasteland towns and cities. All her aspirations dead forever , it broke my heart , it broke my heart.

Something that always renews my hope in humanity is when I see someone save a stranger. A train conductor was once livid at me for paying for someones fare when he wanted to throw the judicial train book at her. The pious judgement of morning talk shows like the most famous hour of hypocritical judgement churned out every day , makes me sick . This man has not struggled he wasn't born into the poverty most of his guests have. He swans around in make up while the guest is shown in there absolute worst light. Picking on his guests who are victims in many ways and struggle to be able to articulate there feelings because of family , social , and all kinds of abuse in their upbringing. He takes great pleasure behind his bodyguards cowardly attacking socially defenceless "guests". A bully of the highest order re-victimising already damaged people is so cowardly and for what entertainment??

A friend of mine attended one of these bear baiting shows and he said the audience were that of an obedient dog. Its like watching the reverend Jim Jones and the peoples temple or David Miscaviage at a Scientology event all over again. Even Jimmy Savile who my grandfather always called "a wrong un" .My grandfather was a rough old bruiser in Leeds who wouldn't take a cross word from anyone. One day my grandfather was doing what he did to get by dealing in horses. He'd been back-kicked several times by a horse and the horse always ended up regretting it. Anyhow "Sir" Jimmy pulled up to my granddad in his Rolls Royce and says taking the piss with a young female passenger no doubt under age. Savile said " I fancy a trade off ha ha" with my granddad in his usual horse an cart. My granddad said one more word out of you and I'll punch your teeth down your throat . It was a different era back then now its subtle and more sophisticated , it always blows me away when people say "in the sixties we never even heard the word paedophile or what it meant" . Because the 70s, 80s, and 90s were there hey day. With groups like P.I.E(paedophile information exchange) making huge strides in all fields of government to legitimise the group and lower the legal age of consent to just 4. We have some of the lowest sentences and convictions for child abuse in the western world. Some of the sentences have been down right ridiculous compared to America who are extremely stringent with sex offenders , over here its like the paedophiles are legislating the law and sentences!

A man naked fully naked walked into a playground in my town and he got away! How?! I was faced with a moral dilemma that I knew I did the right thing. A girl was raped in Britain's first designated red light zone downtown in a subway and the offender EFIT face leapt out at me . It was down to a damn tee, my heart sank I'd seen him drunk an hour before the incident looking very drunk and embittered. The efit scared the living hell out of me, It was his distinctive long hair it was his rodent like features and his signature red hoody he was wearing that night. I knew I had to call so I did but because like in all rape cases unless shes DNA swabbed straight after you have no evidence. Which is why the rape convictions are so horrendously bad and these are only reported cases 9 out of 10 rapes go unreported with the victim so traumatised and irrationally sometimes blaming themselves. So the case was dropped I could never look at him the same again because I just knew. We protect the offender in this country and give no justice to victims and survivors . I'd like to talk to my local MP Ed Milliband about this but all I can find is a run down sign and a run down building you can't enter. Powerful people seem to believe diplomatic immunity runs through their vein's , the jailing of max Clifford seemed more than meets the eye . He was the last free media cowboy basically running an extortion racket with people in the public eyes reputations, someone who could make or break careers over night. They talk as if it was all these yesteryear celebrities to make the public believe 'it went on then, it doesn't go on now'

But it has only gone underground . They all thought they were untouchable and try and say "oh it was the swinging sixties" no it wasn't it was a complete abuse of power and entitlement. Every Hollywood star that doesn't come up through the theatre or the craft pretty much started out as some Hollywood producers sex toy. The state controlling of the press had to be complete by getting rid of a cowboy like max Clifford . I dread for future generations born into shackles they can't even decipher.

There is a sex offender every 10 feet in this town like the analogy of rats in London. Is it nature? Is it nurture? Well its defiantly a mental disease and what do we do with people suffering from violent outbursts of schizophrenia? We keep them in a secure mental hospital , not release them out into the community and just wait for a child to turn up missing. There is so many paedophiles that people don't realise as with gary glitter that they might admire and like them. Underage teenage girls is one thing but 6-8 year olds, that man should be shot for showing zero remorse to his many many victims. Because for many powerful people straight love making isn't good enough , they want something different and that's how the deviancy begins . Political figures , leaders of industry and judges and magistrates can be the worst offenders just as much if not more than working class paedophiles. These rings are self protecting, my heart forever pains for all the kids from all backgrounds children's homes taken never to live out there lives. With the current government it does make you ashamed to be british , ɪ If not abuse a moment ago an abuse 30 years ago,

Lies an abuse and a stain upon a life

Yesterday is Today for abuse goes on forever more

Monsters hiding behind time

Let them see the havoc they have destroyed,

Every moment is history

Just like a murder

The truth shall out

For the victims may the heavens

Bring Justice and harmony to their lives

We have seen the invevitable north of England decimated by the tories we have seen this since I was a newborn baby during the mining strikes. The current austerity measures are nothing more than a continuation tool to dismantle British working class culture even further. All my 30 year life I have witnessed this with the mining conflict and new labour trying to create a new class which has turned out to be an underclass of shocking poverty. The smoking ban has killed the pub industry they used to be booming with vibrancy now everyone has turned in on themselves closed like an impenetrable shell. People should be gven a choice not just ordered these are public houses not pre-schools they just impose there will , we are the masters of our virtues .

Forget culture we see it all blow away to product placement the beautiful music scenes I prey come back., it has all gone . The generation before have not a clue about cultural landmarks that have taken place in the last 100 years. Music for me growing up was 90s which had some great music before it seems popular music has turned into an annoying advert you can't switch off. Of course any scene iv ever witnessed can't rival the 60's and 70's boom periods where a lack of instant gratification technology created more of a frenzy and intrigue, kids shall always have an imagination and the youth shall always need a forum to express themselves. Now exist very hostile clubs where people are very afraid to open up. The main club in this bottomless pit is truly a cess pit meat market of some of the worst behaviour it makes me ashamed to be a man. Literally every girl in the club is groped and sexually assaulted.by steroid induced reprobates without class or a second thought. They swagger around the place looking for sex which they usually can't attain when they open there mouths so they settle with giving an innocent patron usually more vulnerable a brain haemorrhage orphaning there kids the victims just don't stop. This has nothing to do with music anymore, the culture is beating someone more vulnerable than you senseless. The bouncers condone an actively encourage this barbarism I would rather douse myself in sulphuric acid than go to the hell hole clubs of this town.

You've broke my city tonight

Doused my city in filth

No one shall know better

The music is dead

The spirit is gone

All that remains is

SOCIAL UNREST

By the seems by design

I see stock footage of the punk era and wish the kids nowadays could grow a pair and strike back instead of queing for hours for the new IPHONE . Such a depressing sight and sign of the times. That vision makes me so sad its like they feel they have made some kind of achievement buying some stupid piece of metal and plastic. They queue like obedient slaves ready for there moment with god I genuinely find it disturbing the way the youth has been corrupted by meaningless possessions. They don't even realise they've sold there identity down the river for stupid consumer material.

Lets the lemmings march on,

Let the thoughtless lemmings march on without a care

Without a care but the deceitful western world,

Let them walk technologically waiting to die,

Let them not care what goes on in the world,

Let them not care who suffers for their comfort,

Let them walk straight off the cliff

Let them walk straight off the cliff

There is only one occupation around here and that is having unwanted kids for economical reasons, it's a bog standard racket up in this northern English hell. Its used to secure a house, not pay bills, and to avoid work and the kids live in appalling conditions fending for themselves . The bus station for the average person after an hour can be a damaging place , the way the "mothers" treat the kids is unbelievable arguing almost on the same level as the children which tells you something about these mothers intelligence. Its like watching a cycle of victims creating victims creating victims. Racism is also rife you can get seriously hurt just waiting for a damn bus. It disappoints me in this day and age that racism is still alive and kicking. I personally always say a moron's perception of politics is Racism. The towns bus station is rife with a background noise of racial slurs and is genuinely how I imagine hell to be without the fire. Its brutal, the teenagers are beyond stupid and ignorant they can barely string a sentence together. The mothers scream and shriek at a level that makes your stomach turn. The kids being brought up in that obviously become damaged and they go into all manner of mental illness. It tends to make everyone heartless these issues are not going to go away and they need to be addressed because in the end there is always a price to be paid.

I miss genuine culture not this vanilla politically correct excuse, because when there is none the victims just a keep on a coming. It breaks my heart mothers who couldn't care less.

Jail just like America just institutionalises the offender into feeling a permanent dirty failure and sadly that's how you create career criminals. They can't gain employment there sense of providing for there family is gone it really is a crime factory churning them out making hundreds of thousands of pounds in the sickening term "The Prison Industry". It's a wicked cycle— crime creates jobs for police an the many facets of jobs and then private companiess like Serco and G4S make a £150,000 per prisoner from the government , but what they don't tell you is our politicians have shares in these companies its exploitation of the poorest people . Everybody in this town just wants to sedate themselves from the pain of reality, through all manner of downers. Just to escape for a brief moment because there is no way out –educationally or economically. Everything cost exorbitant amounts of money and they lack the people skills to engratiate themselves into other cultures. A great man once said before finding his liberation in life, life was like waiting for a bus that never came. Well its like waiting for a freight train that takes all winter then hits you head on and runs you over.

Its waiting for you kid,

Those demons are always a waiting

Lingering at those gates,

Waiting for you to slip,

And to fall at their Gates , and to fall at there knees

We are currently in a war for the safety of our children, people have to realise just how prevalent this is. It isn't talked about because of an irrational stigma that has gave nothing but a cloak for paedophiles to offend. Paedophiles exist in all social stratospheres its only your rich and influential ones that seem above the law. Again it isn't talked about if people realised how many victims and offenders there are in there life they would be astounded. The "treatment" hasn't worked and we now know the damage sexual abuse causes its time for punishment to be the focus. People are only now be very cautious of there kids whereas before there was an attitude of disbelief like "well you can trust Colin he's such a nice guy and is great with the kids" yes and hes also a convicted child abuser. The old Yorkshire ripper syndrome "oh Petes a family man", yes but he would also go out and kill vulnerable women. The whole of Yorkshire was at a standstill with that now stupid Geordie jack tape playing on loud speakers around neighbourhoods and cinemas . If that would have been London there wud'nt have been an umpteen victim.

We're the forgotten wasteland that's all we are.

Lives discarded by the wayside,

Victims pile beyond any skyline,

Flip a coin for mercy,

Have Your Way But We Shall Never All Be Free

The expenses of MP's in this current climate is obscene these people do not need a hand with money and I don't know how they live with themselves. It's a spit and a slap in the face of every child in poverty in this country. I wish David Cameron could live on £40 a week in Wythenshawe, the largest council estate in Europe. The poor paying for second and third homes is sickening when I see so many families living in poverty as far as the eye can see , I would feel so ashamed if I was them but then again that would require a heart and empathy but they do not possess these quality's as we can see , so by definition they are Sociopathic .

They have no clue about life as we know it no life experience at all. Ian Duncan smith isn't even qualified for goodness sake hes been a failure at every aspect of his life. But hes cutting the disabled's benefits and there replying by killing themselves in their droves . The man has no remorse whatsoever he blanks any questions from any constituents so by definition with his total lack of empathy– this is psychopathy. And sadly there are very few working class members of this rusted bent parliament, so 99.9% of them are just white collar criminals. And we still believe there lies. The distance between the rich and the poor is becoming further and further apart, its time to stop paying there never ending taxes, its time to stop supporting there corporate masters . Shop locally not with there heartless cold corporations stop supporting corporate mainstream supermarkets and rely upon each other economically. Then they shall listen but we must

Come together and stop all the petty bigotry that has divided us for centuries. Its used in all our so called "free media" vilifying people on welfare benefits, gypsies , immigrants to keep us divided blaming each other where the blame lays with all our governments in this case Westminster. Look at where its lead us for gods sake. TOLLERENCE IS THE ONLY WAY FORWARD! We're all suffering but them lets rebuild our community's , lets help all the people suffering right now because those cowards in Westminster are not. We are the human race we've built a civilisation , lets use it to help not destroy people. Its all in the family tell your kids you love them it makes a hell of a difference , when families are together it builds a greater sense of family within the whole society. Kids need to be told imagine if that was your sister or mother or brother because these conditions are producing mentally ill children with No Conscious. The cuts within the public spending and low or in some cases no tax is a good power play, they don't want people focused on politics because then some challenge may present itself. They want you in debt in poverty going to work struggling back an forth like a head less chicken. If they need anything and I do mean anything at all-BOOM! Its there with there expenses paid for by us, We struggle to just simply exist. They promote selfish noncompassionate and borderline sociopathic living. Outlaw the homeless in London for gods sake like these unfortunate souls chose this kind of lifestyle.

MAKE A DIFFERENCE
IN YOUR COMMUNITY
FOR THIS IS YOUR
LIFE,
YOUR WORLD,
YOUR SOCIETY ,
No Matter What They Say,
Bring Some Light
To A Dark World

The most pro-active way is to stop supporting these corporations when you have to. Shop locally stop watching there sophisticated opinion making programming and go outside even the internet has so many thought provoking films to actually enrich your mind .The television is clinging on but its losing credibility by the day , the national terrestrial media has become a national embarrassment now. Issuing a rather silly denial that prince Andrew defiantly hasn't been sleeping with under age girls was a total landmark of humiliation , it defecated on anything resembling journalism / We as a society have to talk amd establish consideration of each other . Don't feed into the Muslim/EDL "debate "Anjem Choudhry declares for a law of murder and breaks every sense of the lawful act of causing racial hatred, but hes in central London preaching everyday why/ Because hes there to antagonise and create tension between Muslims and non Muslims . Most Muslims see him as a joke but while white people become aggressive - here in lays the problem. Always Anyone who brought people together was violently killed in one way or another. Anjem Choudhry seems to be some kind of hate figure for closet racists to flip there lid . WE MUST STICK TOGETHER ! This is our land we know better than the old divide and conquer trick . Its time if you love your wife or your children we have to say no to the mass corruption at any levels and really support any rallies or showing up on a crucial day and really demonstrating mass strikes to show we have the power also. We have an old rusted 60s,70s government full of disgusting perverts still being protected today . This has truly got to change but not only government but the security services are completely out of control.

Anyone who brought people together was violently killed in one way or another. Anjem Choudhry seems to be some kind of hate figure for closet racists to flip there lid . WE MUST STICK TO-GETHER ! This is our land we know better than the old divide and conquer trick . Its time if you love your wife or your children we have to say no to the mass corruption at any levels and really support any rallies or showing up on a crucial day and really demonstrating mass strikes to show we have the power also. We have an old rusted 60s,70s government full of disgusting perverts still being protected today . This has truly got to change but not only government but the security services are completely out of control.

www.ingramcontent.com/pod-product-compliance
Lightning Source LLC
Chambersburg PA
CBHW070523290526
45790CB00003B/1278